THE FAR SIDE GALLERY 2

Other Books in The Far Side Series

The Far Side
Beyond The Far Side
In Search of The Far Side
Bride of The Far Side
Valley of The Far Side
Hound of The Far Side
It Came from The Far Side
The Far Side Observer
Night of the Crash-Test Dummies
Wildlife Preserves
Wiener Dog Art
Unnatural Selections

Anthologies

The Far Side Gallery
The Far Side Gallery 3

The Prehistory of The Far Side:
A 10th Anniversary Exhibit

THE FAR SIDE GALLERY 2

by Gary Larson

WARNER BOOKS

A *Warner* Book

Copyright © 1984, 1985, 1986 by Universal Press Syndicate;
Copyright © 1980, 1981, 1982, 1983, 1984 by the Chronicle Publishing Company

First published by Futura Publications in 1989
Reprinted 1989 (twice), 1990 (twice), 1991 (twice)

This edition published by Warner Books in 1992
Reprinted 1992

ISBN 0 7515 0237 5

Printed and bound in Great Britain by
The Guernsey Press Company Limited, Guernsey, Channel Islands

Warner Books
A Division of
Little, Brown and Company (UK) Limited
165 Great Dover Street
London SE1 4YA

On The Far Side

Wanna hear my definition of a Golden Age as applies to *x*?

No?

Okay, here it is anyway: A Golden Age is a time when so many things about *x* are wonderful and unique that *x* itself is taken for granted.

And you can quote me, honeychile.

Take the art of cartooning in the '80s.

I could say that the work of Gary Larson is absolutely unique, and that it will make you laugh your butt off, and that is true, but it means nothing in itself because in the '80s there are at least *two dozen* cartoonists who can make you laugh your butt off, and *all* of them are unique. We are living in the Golden Age of print cartoons, friends and neighbors, and the Q.E.D. of the postulate is that we simply take them for granted: Jim (Garfield) Davis, Charles (Charlie) Rodrigues, Charles (Peanuts) Schulz, Garry (Doonesbury) Trudeau, Berke (Bloom County) Breathed . . . and those are just for starters.

Gary Larson, however, is *uniquely* unique.

You can mention other cartoonists of the surreal — Charles Addams, Gahan Wilson, Virgil Partch — but Larson is as different from all of them as they are from him.

You want me to tell you why?

I *can't* tell you why.

There's no way to explain humor any more than there is a way to explain horror, which is probably why a man like Larson (or Addams, or Wilson, or Rodrigues) must hear the question I often hear so many times: *Where do you get your ideas?*

My answer is Utica.

It doesn't mean anything, but I don't know the answer, and at least it shuts 'em up.

I don't know what Larson's answer is.

And it doesn't matter. Either these cartoons will do it for you or they will not, just as anchovies do it for some people and other people won't touch them — find them, in fact, so revolting that they will commit the impoliteness of wondering aloud why other people eat them.

It's just a taste you can't explain.

You can't "tell" a cartoon; if you could, cartoonists would be out of business. A cartoon isn't simply a joke; it's a talented eye combining circumstance and joke in a clearly recognizable way which cannot be duplicated. You could copy Gary Larson's pictures, just as you could copy Charles Schulz's round-headed worrywart, Charlie Brown; it's Larson's *mind* which makes him one of a kind.

Having said that you can't tell a cartoon, let me tell you my favorite Gary Larson cartoon (and I only do it because I've previewed the book which follows

5

and believe this cartoon isn't in it, unless it is a late add):

Two dogs are in a den. One is showing the other his trophies. One trophy is that part of the human anatomy which exists south of the wrist. "And *that* one is the hand that fed me," the dog is saying (and speaking, one somehow assumes, in the bored but privileged tones of a British *burra sahib* at the height of the Indian *raj*).

This cartoon *alone* only made me smile. But the effect of Larson's work, unlike that of many surreal cartoonists (I except only Gahan Wilson from the general rule), is *cumulative*. I found myself not looking at these circumstantial jokes as single things, isolated from one another; they seem somehow connected, and they certainly had a cumulative effect on me, as did my Larson day-by-day calendar. You start smiling; then you're grinning; then you start to giggle; then you start to laugh; then you begin to howl; finally you are lying on the floor, hoping to God you won't have a hernia or a heart attack, telling yourself to *stop*, for God's sake *stop looking at them*, but you go along just the same, because he's drawn you into a unique Larsonian world where deer talk with an oddly persuasive matter-of-factness; where Godzilla drives a Plymouth with a license plate reading I 8 NY, one arm cocked out the window, smiling grimly; where a crazed flea marches through hairs the size of Sequoias holding up a sign which reads THE END OF THE DOG IS COMING! It's all insane *but you can't stop*.

But that's good, because in the end you feel better. Why? Don't ask me. Don't say things like *catharsis* or *reductio ad absurdum* or *surrealism*. Cartooning is art, and I don't know doodly-squat about art. Like the rock song says, "I ain't no monkey, but I know what I like." And I like Gary Larson a lot, partly because he turns the world as I know it inside out like a sock, partly because he turns the world as I know it into a funhouse mirror, but mostly because he does what artists and humorists are supposed to do: he sees what I would see if I could have his eyes. I don't have them, but thank God they are on loan.

Like a chill in a dark place, good cartoons are a momentary *frisson*; they are a hit like a drug that is addicting but does no damage; does, in fact, good.

Explain him?

No.

Explicate him?

No.

Enjoy him?

Yes.

God, yes.

Forget the anchovies on your pizza; if you can dig anchovies of the *mind*, you're gonna have a *blast*.

Just don't o.d.

You could die laughing.

STEPHEN KING

"You gotta check this out, Stuart. Vinnie's over on the couch putting the moves on Zelda Schwartz—but he's talkin' to the wrong end."

"Well, I suppose you're all wondering why I've asked you here today. ... Ha! I've always wanted to say that."

"Gad, it gives me the creeps when he does that. I swear that goldfish is possessed or something."

"Don't shush me—and I don't care if she IS writing in her little notebook; just tell me where you were last night!"

Eventually, Murray took the job—but his friends never did speak to him again.

"Well, we must face a new reality. No more carefree days of chasing squirrels, running through the park, or howling at the moon. On the other hand, no more 'Fetch the stick, boy, fetch the stick.'"

"Here, Fifi! C'mon! ... Faster, Fifi!"

"Hank! You're reflecting!"

"Cummings! Schneider! You've got plenty of research to work on ... and for the last time stop making those plastic models fight."

Dreaming he's falling, Jerry forgets the well-known "always-wake-up-before-you-land" rule.

"Well, I'm not sure. ... You don't carry any other styles?"

"You idiot! I said get the room freshener! That's the insecticide!"

When careers and allergies collide

How vampires have accidents

"Guess who!"

"Mom! Theron's dried his bed again."

One day, as he nonchalantly reaches for a match, Leonardo da Vinci's life is suddenly transformed.

Danny shows off his sheep's brain.

Across town in the snake district

"Me? I WAS charging on the right, when you suddenly went left, so I went left, and then you went right again, you idiot!"

"Well, I don't think so, but I'll ask. Hey, Arlene! Anyone turn in a human brain left here yesterday? ... He says it was medium-sized, sort of pinkish."

"Hold on there! I think you misunderstood—I'm Al Tilley ... the bum."

"Just stay in the cab, Vern ... maybe that bear's hurt, and maybe he ain't."

Suddenly the burglars found themselves looking down the barrel of Andy's Dobie-o-matic.

"You know those teeny tiny little birds that walk around so trustingly inside a crocodile's mouth? Well, I just been eatin' those little guys like popcorn."

The morning dew sparkled on Bill's web. The decoys were in place, his fly call was poised, and luck was in the air.

"If there're monsters moving in next door, Danny, you just ignore them. The more you believe in them, the more they'll try to get you."

"Well, if you're almost ready, *I'm* dressed to kill."

Saturday morning in the Garden

In the animal self-help section

"It's the mailman, doc. He scares me."

"Once in a while couldn't we just have some pasta?"

Belly button slipknots

"Foster! You better get over here if you want to see Johnson's hangnail magnified 500 times."

"Well, I beg your pardon. ... But where I come from, it's considered a compliment to let fly with a good trumpeting after dinner."

"Randy's goin' down!"

"Yes ... I believe there's a question there in the back."

"Look out, Larry! ... That retriever has finally found you!"

The fords of Norway

"Your room is right in here, Maestro."

"Wendell ... I'm not content."

"Well, okay, Frank. ... Maybe it IS just the wind."

"Oh, yeah? If you're alone, then whose eye is *that?*"

"Bob, do you think I'm sinking? Be honest."

Harold would have been on his guard, but he thought the old gypsy woman was speaking figuratively.

"Yup. This year they're comin' along reeeeeeal good. ... Course, you can always lose a few to an early frost or young pups."

As Harriet turned the page, a scream escaped her lips: There was Donald—his strange disappearance no longer a mystery.

Disaster befalls Professor Schnabel's cleaning lady when she mistakes his time machine for a new dryer.

Sixty-five million years ago, when cows ruled the earth

Invertebrate practical jokes

"Open the gate! It's a big weiner dog!"

26

"Polly wanna finger."

"I've seen this sort of thing before, Baxter ... and it's *not* a pretty sight."

"Just pull it off and apologize, Cromwell ... or we'll go out in the hall and establish this pecking order once and for all!"

"The fuel light's on, Frank! We're all going to die! ... We're all going to die! ... Wait, wait. ... Oh, my mistake—that's the intercom light."

"See how the vegetation has been trampled flat here, Jimmy? That tells me where a deer bedded down for the night. After a while, you'll develop an eye for these things yourself."

"C'mon, c'mon, buddy! The heart! Hand over the heart! ... And you with the brains! ... Let's have 'em!"

This time I won't screw up! I won't, I won't, I won't, I won't...

Roger screws up.

A lucky night for Goldy

The modern lion

"Hold on there, Dale. It says we should sand
between coats."

"Hey! ... You kids!"

Late at night, his own stomach would foil Gordon's attempt at dieting.

"Bob! You fool. ... Don't plug that thing in!"

In the days before soap

Common medieval nightmare

"For crying out loud, Doris. ... You gotta drag that thing out *every* time we all get together?"

"I'm leaving you, Charles ... and I'm taking the grubs with me."

Aerobics in hell

Andrew is hesitant, remembering his fiasco with the car of straw.

Animal game shows

"He's using blanks—pass it on."

"Be back by suppertime, Hump … and, as always, you be careful."

Einstein discovers that time is actually money.

"And the next thing I knew, the whole ship just sunk right out from under me. So what's the deal with you? ... You been here long or what?"

Suddenly, everything froze. Only the buzzing of the tsetse flies could be heard. The crackling grass wasn't Cummings returning to camp after all, but an animal who didn't like to be surprised.

The livestock would gather every morning, hoping for one of Farmer Dan's popular "airplane" rides.

The rhino in repose

"Never mind the name. You just tell your boss some *thing* is here to see him!"

"Well, I guess that ain't a bad story—but let me tell you about the time I lost *this!*"

The squid kids at home

"And as the net sloooooowly lifted him from the water, the voice kept whispering, 'I want your legs. … I want your legs.'"

Down at the Eat and Slither

"Oo! Goldfish, everyone! Goldfish!"

Butterflies from the wrong side of the meadow

"Uh-oh, I've got a feeling I shouldn't have been munching on these things for the last mile."

Charles wanders into a herd of dirt buffaloes.

As the smallest member of the gang, Wendall was used as an attention-getter while cruising for girls.

"One more thing, young man. You get my daughter home before sunrise—I don't want you coming back here with a pile of dried bones."

"You're gonna be OK, mister, but I can't say the same for your little buddy over there. ... The way I hear it, he's the one that mouthed off to them gunfighters in the first place."

"Thunderstick? ... You actually said, 'Thunderstick?' ...
That, my friend, is a Winchester 30.06."

Vending machines of the Serengeti

"Well, somehow they knew we were—whoa! Our dorsal
fins are sticking out! I wonder how many times *that's*
screwed things up?"

"My turn. ... Well, I'm originally from the shores of the
upper Nile and ... saaaaaay. ... Did anyone ever tell
you your pupils are ROUND?"

"Barrow"—precursor to the game of "wheelbarrow"

"To the death, Carlson! Hang on to the death!"

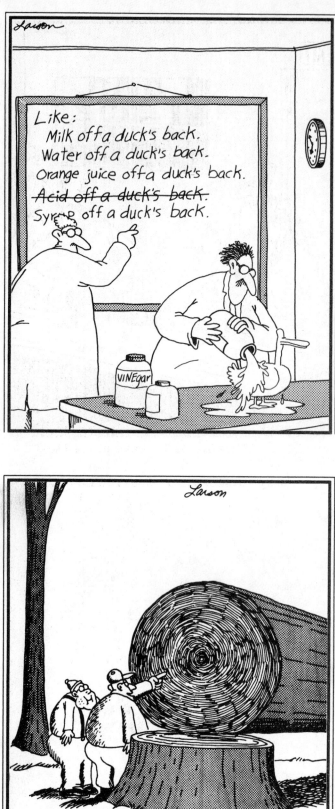

Like:
Milk off a duck's back.
Water off a duck's back.
Orange juice off a duck's back.
~~Acid off a duck's back.~~
Syrup off a duck's back.

VINEgar

"Say … wasn't there supposed to be a couple of holes punched in this thing?"

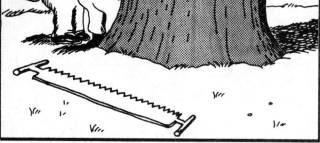

"And see this ring right here, Jimmy? … That's another time when the old fellow miraculously survived some big forest fire."

Deep inside, Brian wondered if the other guys really listened to his ideas or regarded him only as comic relief.

"Well, every dog has his day."

"Oh yeah? More like the three wise guys, I'd say."

When animal mimicry breaks down

"C'mon, c'mon! You've done this a hundred times, Uzula; the vines *always* snap you back just before you hit. ... Remember, that's *National Geographic* down there."

Carl Sagan as a kid

"Nothing yet. ... How about you, Newton?"

Early experiments in transportation

"Well, we just took the wrong exit. I know this breed, Morrison—you have to watch them every minute or wham, they'll turn on you."

"I knew it! I just knew it ... 'Shave-and-a-Haircut' was a lousy secret knock."

"Rusty! Two points!"

"Well, there it goes again. ... And we just sit here without opposable thumbs."

"Now listen! You both know the rules, you've got equal portions, and we're going to settle this thing once and for all ... On your mark ... Get set ..."

"Now remember—roar just as you leap. ... These things have some of the greatest expressions."

"Well, Bobby, it's not like you haven't been warned. ... No roughhousing under the hornet's nest!"

"Wait a minute, Stan. ... These are good hubcaps. If we don't take 'em, it's a cinch some other bears will."

"I don't seeeeee. ... Wait! There it is! Oo! I hate those little slivers that stand straight up and down."

"Sorry, mister ... but this is what we do to cattle rustlers in these parts."

"Excuse me, but I'm trying to sleep next door and all I hear is scratching, clawing, and 'eek, eek, eek.'"

"I just CAN'T go in there, Bart! ... Some fellow in there and I are wearing the same hat!"

"Just a minute, young man! ... What are you taking from the jungle?"

"Gee ... look at all the little black dots."

"Fuel ... check. Lights ... check. Oil pressure ... check. We've got clearance. OK, Jack—let's get this baby off the ground."

"What is this? ... Some kind of cruel hoax?"

"… four … five … six … Oh, what the hell—just turn and shoot."

"I just can't tell from here. … That could either be our flock, another flock, or just a bunch of little m's"

The Holsteins visit the Grand Canyon.

"It's Henderson again, sir. ... He always faints at the sight of yolk."

Farmer Brown froze in his tracks; the cows stared wide-eyed back at him. Somewhere, off in the distance, a dog barked.

"Bedtime, Leroy. Here comes your animal blanket."

"*Now* that desk looks better. Everything's squared away, yessir, squaaaaaared away."

"Hey! C'mon! Hold it! Hold it! ... Or someone's going to get hurt."

Toby vs. Godzilla

"Sorry ... we're dead."

"Yes, with the amazing new 'knife,' you only have to wear the SKIN of those dead animals."

"And, if you squint your eyes just right, you can see the zork in the earth."

"Criminy! Kevin's oozing his way up onto the table. ...
Some slugs have a few drinks and just go nuts!"

"Saaaaaay, aren't you a stranger in these parts? Well, I don't *take* candy from *strangers*."

"For crying out loud! ... We were supposed to turn south after that last mountain range!"

Randy and Mark were beginning to sense the wolves were up to no good.

"Great ... Just great, you imbecile! I've been floating here for hours like a harmless log and *you* come up and start talking to me!"

"This was *your* suggestion, Edna! ... 'Let's play Twister, everyone, let's play Twister!'"

Tempers flare when Professors Carlson and Lazzell, working independently, ironically set their time machines to identical coordinates.

"Get, you rascal! Get! ... Heaven knows how he keeps getting in here,
Betty, but you better count 'em."

Garbage dumps of the wild

"Well, shucks! I've lost again. Talk about your alien luck!"

"Trim the bowl, you idiots! Trim the bowl!"

Primitive peer pressure

"Dang! Get my shotgun, Mama! The aliens are after the chickens again."

"Looks like the bank's been hit again. Well, no hurry—we'll take the big horse."

At Maneaters Anonymous

"You know, I have a confession to make, Bernie. Win or lose, I love doing this."

Unfortunately, Larry had always approached from the side that wasn't posted, and a natural phenomenon was destroyed before anyone could react.

"There it is—the old Muffy place. They say on some nights, when the moon is full, you can still hear him dragging his chain to the old oak and back."

PRISON
for the
MENTALLY
DERANGED

Attaaaaaaack!

Ivan! You're out!

Simon says... Attaaaaaaack!

The origin of "dessert"

"Well, Zoron. ... Is THIS a close enough look for you?"

"The picture's pretty bleak, gentlemen. ... The world's climates are changing, the mammals are taking over, and we all have a brain about the size of a walnut."

"Let's see here. ... Oh! Close, but no cigar. You want the place up the road—same as I told those other fellahs."

"And I suppose *you* think this is a dream come true."

Wild parakeets

"Shh. Listen! There's more: 'I've named the male with the big ears Bozo, and he is surely the nerd of the social group—a primate bimbo, if you will.'"

"That's right, the forty-ninth floor. . . . And you better hurry— she's hanging by a thread."

"... And once, when I was a kid, a lion chased me up that old acacia... I used to swing on those vines all day long... Gee, all the trees seem so much smaller to me now.

Tarzan visits his childhood home.

"Ha ha ha, Biff. Guess what? After we go to the drugstore and the post office, *I'm* going to the vet's to get tutored."

"Mom! Edgar's making that clicking sound again!"

"Grunt, snort ... grunt grunt, snort ..."

"Puuuuut the caaaaat ouuuuuuuuut ... Puuuuut the caaaaat ouuuuuuut ..."

"Hey, thank you! Thank you! That was 'Tie a Yellow Ribbon.' ... Now, what say we all *really* get down?"

"Sorry to intrude, ma'am, but we thought we'd come in and just sort of roam around for a few minutes."

"C'mon, Arlene. Just a few feet in and then we can stand."

"Just back off, buddy ... unless you want a fat lip."

"I beg your pardon, but you're not planning just to throw that fly away, are you?"

The Great Nerd Drive of '76

"Now, I want you all to know this cat's *not* from the market—Rusty caught it himself."

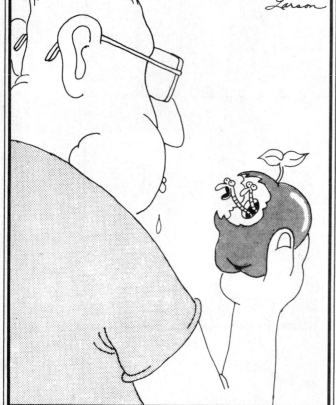

"Egad! ... It's got Uncle Jake!"

"The big fellah's gonna be A-OK, Mrs. Dickerson. Now, a *square* knot would've been bad news, but this just appears to be a 'granny.'"

In God's kitchen

Suddenly, Bobby felt very alone in the world.

"Rise and shine, everyone! ... It's a beautiful day and we're all going to the window sill."

Carrots of the evening

The nightmare makers

History and the snake

"I assume you're being facetious, Andrews ... I distinctly yelled 'second' before you did."

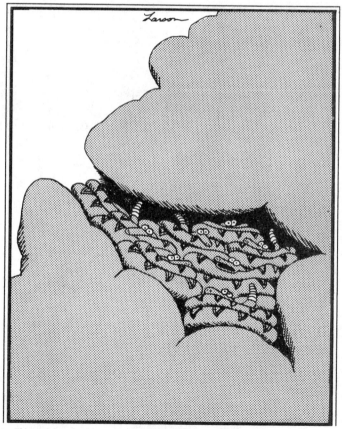

"Hey, I feel someone moving! Dang, this place gives me the willies."

Stupid clerks

The young dog's nightmare: premature mange

The shark on the go

Tarzan contemplates another entry.

Testing the carnivore-proof vest

The bride, best man, and ushers of Frankenstein

Nanoonga froze—worrying less about ruining a good head than he did the social faux pas.

Creationism explained

"Remember me, Mr. Schneider? Kenya. 1947. If you're going to shoot at an elephant, Mr. Schneider, you better be prepared to finish the job."

Knowing how it could change the lives of canines everywhere, the dog scientists struggled diligently to understand the Doorknob Principle.

"Sorry about this, buddy, but the limit on those things is half a dozen—looks like you're one over."

"So, Billy! Seems your father and I can never leave without you getting yourself into some kind of trouble!"

"As if we all knew where we're going."

"You're on. Ten to one if I start howling I'll have everyone here howling inside five minutes."

At the rubber man factory

"Well, you better get someone over here right away. ....
He really looks like he's going to jump."

"And here he is—but when I started, I bet he was at least
this tall."

"Ha! Ain't a rattler, Jake. You got one of them maraca
players down your bag—and he's probably more scared
than you."

84

Duggy's science project gets in Mr. Og's hair.

Cheetah wheelies

"Listen! The authorities are helpless! If the city's to be saved, I'm afraid it's up to us! *This is our hour!*"

"Thag, take napkin. Got some mammoth on face."

"Now watch this. He'll keep that chicken right there until I say OK. ... You wanna say OK, Ernie?"

Hour after hour, cup after cup, the two men matched their caffeine limits in a traditional contest of the Old West.

At the Comedians' Cemetery

"Oh, quit worrying about it, Andrew. They're just love handles."

Hit elephants

"My next guest, on the monitor behind me, is an organized crime informant. To protect his identity, we've placed him in a darkened studio—so let's go to him now."

Ginger decides to take out Mrs. Talbot's flower bed once and for all.

"Aaaaaa! Here they come again, Edgar! ... Crazy carnivores!"

How entomologists pass away

Canine social blunders

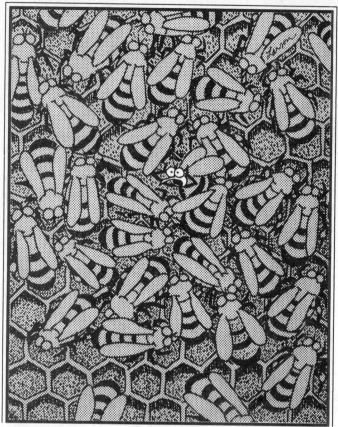

"No more! No more! I can't take it! ... That incessant buzzing sound!"

"Mom! Allen's makin' his milk foam!"

The heartbreak of remoras

"Dang it, Monica! I can't live this charade any longer! I'm not a telephone repairman who stumbled into your life— I'm a Komodo dragon, largest member of the lizard family and a filthy liar."

"My word! I'd hate to be caught outside on a day like this!"

How nature says, "Do not touch."

As Thak worked frantically to start a fire, a Cro-Magnon man, walking erect, approached the table and simply gave Theena a light.

"Hey! You'll get a kick out of this, Bob and Ruth! ... Watch what Lola here does with her new squeeze doll!"

French mammoth

The invaluable lizard setter

"Dad! Find out if they have cable!"

"*There's* one of 'em! ... And I think there are at least three or four more runnin' around in here!"

Primitive spelling bees

"There! There! See it, Larry? ... It moved a little closer!"

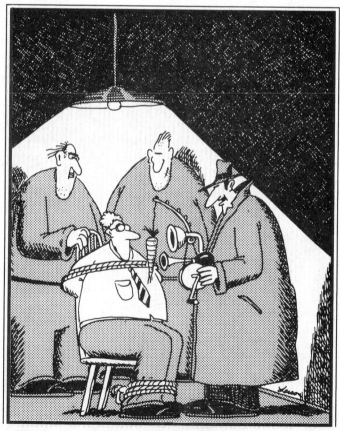

"Well, we've tried every device and you still won't talk—every device, that is, except this little baby we simply call 'Mr. Thingy.'"

"Oh, is that so? Well, you might be a kangaroo, but I know a few things about marsupials *myself*!"

"Hey! I think you've hit on something there! Sheep's clothing! Sheep's clothing! ... Let's get out of these gorilla suits!"

"Mom! He's doing it again!"

"I've got an idea. ... How many here have ever seen Alfred Hitchcock's *The Birds*?"

"Hey, you stupid bovines! You'll never get that contraption off the ground! ... Think it'll run on hay? ... Say, maybe you'll make it to the moooooooon! ..."

"Looks like another one of those stupid 'Incredible Journey' things."

The Vikings, of course, knew the importance of stretching before an attack.

"Feeding frenzy!"

"Hey, hey, hey! Are you folks nuts? I'm telling you, *this* is the car for you."

"Good heavens, Charles! You're at it again! ... And with my fresh sponge cake, I see!"

When worlds collide

"All right! All right! If you want the truth, off and on I've been seeing *all* the vowels—a, e, i, o, u. ... Oh, yes! And *sometimes* y!"

"Ladies! Ladies! He's back! ... Our mystery man who does the Donald Duck impression!"

"Come and get it! Cooooome and get it! ... It's not going to get any more raw, y'know."

"Well, here's your problem, Mr. Schueler."

"For crying out loud, gentlemen! That's us! Someone's installed the one-way mirror in backward!"

When cliff divers belly flop

"Well, here we all are at the Grand Canyon. ... But, as usual, Johnny just had to ruin the picture for everyone else."

"You know, Bjorg, there's something about holding a good, solid mace in your hand—you just look for an excuse to smash something."

The 100-meter mosey

"Louise! C'mon over here. ... I think we might have some bug spreadin' through the store."

"So when Farmer Bob comes through the door, three of us circle around and ... Muriel! ... Are you chewing your cud while I'm talking?"

Fire is invented.

Whenever geese pass through tunnels

The boy who cried "no brakes"

"Now, in this slide we can see how the cornered cat has seemed to suddenly grow bigger. ... Trickery! Trickery! Trickery!"

Animal nerds

Early vegetarians returning from the kill

"Cannonbaaaaaaaallllllllll!"

"Check this guy out, Lois. ... Artificial for sure."

"Okay! I'll talk! I'll talk! ... Take two sticks of
approximately equal size and weight—rub them together
at opposing angles using short, brisk strokes ..."

Life on cloud eight

"And now Edgar's gone. ... Something's going on around here."

When snakes try to chew gum and crawl at the same time

"Well there is some irony in all this, you know ... I mean we BOTH lose a lens at the same time?!!"

"I'm leaving you, Frank, because you're a shiftless, low-down, good-for-nothing imbecile ... and, might I finally add, you have the head of a chicken."

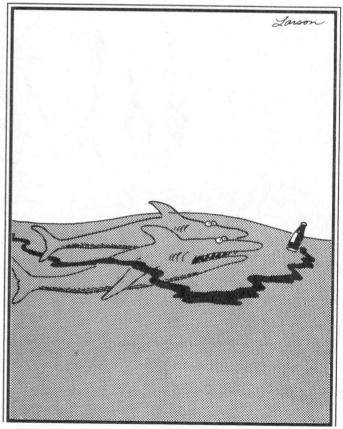

"What the—? Ketchup? We followed a *ketchup* trail for three miles?"

Ed and Barbara are visited by the insects of the
Amazon Basin.

"Look at this mob. We'll be lucky if there's a seat
cushion left."

"Mind if we check the ears?"

Fly heaven

"First!"

Gross stories

How snakes say goodbye

Early musical chairs

The restless life of the nomad

Single-cell sitcoms

Shark nerds always ran the projector.

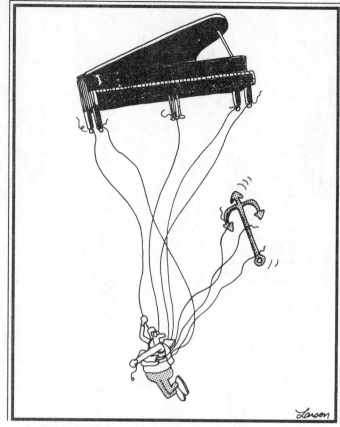

Murray didn't feel the first pangs of real panic until he pulled the emergency cord.

"Hey! I can hear the traffic!"

"Well, here comes Roy again. He sure does think he's Hell on Wheels."

Elephant skyways

"Igor! Get that Wolfman doll out of his face! ... Boy, sometimes you really are bizarre."

"Well, Mr. Cody, according to our questionnaire, you would probably excel in sales, advertising, slaughtering a few thousand buffalo, or market research."

"Well, the Parkers are dead. ... You had to encourage them to take thirds, didn't you?"

"Oooo! Oooo! ... Are you a good witch or a bad witch?"

Billy leaves home to join the zoo, but returns the next day after being told that, as an animal, he was just "too common."

"Bear! Bear!"

As quickly as it had started, the egg fight was over.

"Hey, Barry—in the back row—new kid."

Pirate school

"Well, I've got your final grades ready, although I'm afraid not everyone here will be moving up."

"And now. ... Can dogs really talk? ... We found one who's willing to try, right after this message."

"Hey! ... Six eyes!"

"Look, just relax, son ... relaaaaaaaaax ... I'm gonna come over there now and you can just hand me your gun. ... Everything's gonna be reeeal cool, son."

"Listen ... I'm fed up with this 'weeding out the sick and the old' business ... I want something in its prime."

The anthropologist's dream: A beautiful woman in one hand, the fossilized skull of a *Homo habilus* in the other

118

Circa 1500 A.D.: Horses are introduced to America.

When a tree falls in the forest and no one is around.

"Python ... and he's home."

"Oh, Laaaaaarrrrrry ... I think you should look up niiiiiice and eaaaaasy and see what's right ... over ... your ... head."

"Now calm down, Barbara. ... We haven't looked everywhere yet, and an elephant can't hide forever."

"I see your little, petrified skull ... labeled and resting on a shelf somewhere."

"Say, there's something wrong here. ... We may have to move shortly."

"Harold! The dog's trying to blow up the house again! Catch him in the act or he'll never learn."

"Well, there it goes again. ... Every night when we bed down, that confounded harmonica starts in."

Igor goes shopping.

Childhood innocence

"Oh, that's so disgusting—I guess a fly strip and you in the same house just aren't going to work out."

"It's OK! It's OK! The tunnel was closing in on me there for a while, but I'm all right now."

"Hey. .... Be cool, man, be cool."

Where the buffalo cruise

"What have I told you about eating in bed?"

"Wait a minute! Isn't anyone here a real sheep?"

"Watch ... Thag says he make gravel angel."

"Oh, I see! You return covered with blond feathers, and I'm supposed to believe you crossed the road *just* to get to the other side?"

In his heart, Willy knew the ants were being very foolish.

Thwarting the vampcow

"Take me to your stove? ...You idiot! Give me that book back!"

"Well, we might as well put it on board—although I'm not sure what use we'll have for a box of rusty nails, broken glass, and throwing darts."

"Well, heaven knows what it is or where it came from—
just get rid of it. But save that cheese first."

"It's the Websters. They say there's some pitiful thing dying
of thirst out their way, and would we like to come over?"

Early business failures

"You idiot! ... Now this time wait for me to finish the first
'row, row, row your boat' BEFORE you come in!"

Early Pleistocene mermaids

"Hey! I'm gonna roll now! You guys gonna watch or what?"

"Don't listen to him, George. He didn't catch it. ... The stupid thing swerved to miss him and ran into a tree."

Unwittingly, Irwin has a brush with Death.

"Hold up, Niles. It says here, 'These little fish have been known to skeletonize a cow in less than two minutes.' ... Now there's a vivid thought."

"Shoot! You not only got the wrong planet, you got the wrong solar system ... I mean, a wrong planet I can understand—but a whole solar system?"

"Well, I dunno, Warren ... I think your feet may be uglier than mine."

"Oh, look, Roger! Nerds! ... And some little nerdlings!"

"Oo! Watch out! ... The walls are pointy!"

"Hold still, Omar. ... Now look up. Yep. You've got something in your eye, all right—could be sand."

Punk porcupines

Neanderthal creativity

"Well, I guess I'll have the ham and eggs."

Hank knew this place well. He need only wait. ... The deer would come, the deer would come.

"Well, you've got quite an infestation here, ma'am ... I can't promise anything, but I imagine I can knock out some of the bigger nests."

"Oo, Sylvia! You've got to see this! ... Ginger's bringing Bobby home, and even though her jaws can crush soup bones, Bobby only gets a few nicks and scratches."

"Oh, what a cute little Siamese. ... Is he friendly?"

How locusts are incited to swarm

Practical jokes of the wild

"I tell you she's drivin' me nuts! ... I come home at night
and it's 'quack quack quack' ... I get up in the morning
and it's 'quack quack quack.'"

"Boy, I'm sooooo full, and this is the laaaaast slice of beef ... guess I'll finish it off, though."

"Well, it just sort of wriggled its way up the beach, grabbed Jonathan, and dragged him back again. I mean, the poor thing must have been half-starved."

The termite queen in her egg chamber

Edgar finds his purpose.

"You have to prime it, you know."

"Well, you've overslept and missed your vine again."

"Well, she's done it to me again ... tuna fish!"

Cattle hustler

"*That's* him! *That's* the one! ... I'd recognize that silly little hat *anywhere*!"

"Now you listen to me, Miss Billings! You have not seen a thing here—do you understand? I'm not kidding about this, Miss Billings."

Dinosaur cranial capacity

"Spiders, scorpions, and insecticides, oh my! ... Spiders, scorpions, and insecticides, oh my! ..."

"That's the third one you've lost this month, Edgar. ... You've got to stop believing these guys who say they're just stepping out to use the restroom."

Eventually, Stevie looked up: His mother was nowhere in sight, and this was certainly no longer the toy department.

"Well, *I'm* addicted. ... Have you tried Carol's sheep dip?"

Unfair animal names

tsetse fly

bullhead

booby

platypus

sapsucker

clarence

And then, the dawn is still again—and another miracle of nature emerges.

"Civilization-slickers."

When fleas go unchecked

"Whoa! This just looks like regular spaghetti! ... Where's my Earthworms Alfredo?"

Birds of prey know they're cool.

"Don't be 'fraid, Dug. Me teach him sit on finger. ...
Closer, Dug, closer."

Interplanetary luggage mix-ups

Animal lures

Working alone, Professor Dawson stumbles into a bad
section of the petri dish.

"Oh! Wait! Wait! My mistake! ... That's him down there!"

"Oh, give me a home, where the buffalo roam ..."

"You know, it's really dumb to keep this right next to the cereal. ... In fact, I don't know why we even keep this stuff around in the first place."

Returning from vacation, Roy and Barbara find their house, their neighborhood, their friends—in fact, all of Atlantis—just plain gone.

"Now just hold your horses, everyone. ... Let's let it run for a minute or so and see if it gets any colder."

Mitch loses a dollar.

Harvesting the work of ketchup bees

Unwittingly, Palmer stepped out of the jungle and into headhunter folklore forever.

One remark led to another, and the bar suddenly polarized into two angry, confrontational factions: those espousing the virtues of the double-humped camel on the one side, single-humpers on the other.

Animal samaritans

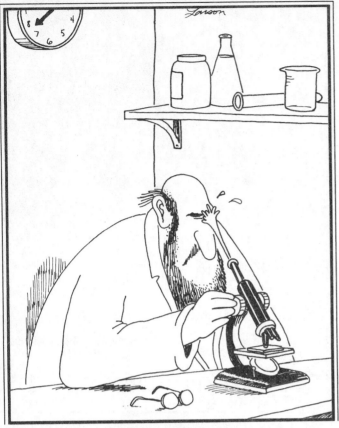

Paramecium humor

"Yes! Yes! This is it, Sidney! The guy with the dog! ... I think he sees us!"

"OK, listen up! The cops are closing in on this place, so here's our new hideout: 455 Elm Street. ... Let's all say it together about a hundred times so there'll be no screw-ups."

"Wait a minute! Just wait a minute! No need to worry. ... According to this, we're dealing with a rhino MIMIC!"

"Look out, Thak! It's a ... a ... dang! Never can pronounce those things!"

"Good heavens—just *look* at you! You've been down at the Ferguson's porch light,
haven't you?"

"No doubt about it, Ellington—we've mathematically expressed
the purpose of the universe. Gad, how I love the thrill
of scientific discovery!"

"For the one-hundredth time in as many days! ... I HAVEN'T GOT A QUARTER!"

"What the ... ANOTHER little casket!!?"

"C'mon, c'mon—it's either one or the other."

"Late again! ... This better be good!"

"Fire!"

"Say, Carl ... forget the Hendersons for a second and come look at this thing."

"Gee whiz ... you mean I get a THIRD wish, too?"

"Take this handkerchief back to the lab, Stevens. I want some answers on which monster did this—Godzilla? Gargantua? Who?"

"C'mon, Gordy. ... Are you *really* choking, or just turning green?"

"For heaven's sake, Elroy! ... NOW look where the earth is! ... Move over and let me drive!"

"Okay, Wellington. I'm comfortable with my grip if you are. ... Have you made a wish?"

When vultures dream

March 5, 1984: After several months, I now feel that these strange little rodents have finally accepted me as one of their own.

"Uh-uh-uh-uh-uh. ... Question. Can anyone here tell me what Hanson there is doing wrong with his elbows?"

When snakes trip

"Oh, wow! How could you even *think* that, Wendy? Of *course* it's your mind I'm attracted to!"

"Well, Vern, looks like that buffalo paper you set out this morning is doing the trick."

"A cat killer? Is that the face of a cat killer? Cat *chaser* maybe. But hey—who isn't?"

"Well, so that's it. ... I thought he was coming up awfully easy."

"OK. Here's another little ditty we can all sing. ... Of course, as always, the only words are 'ribbit, ribbit.'"

"Now you've done it!"

"Aaaaaaa! ... It's George! He's taking it with him!"

Snake dreams

"These little ones are mice. ... These over here are hamsters. ... Ooh! This must be a gerbil!"

"According to the map, this should be the place—but it sure don't look right to me. ... Well, we're supposed to die around here *somewhere*."

Still in its early stages, the Olduvai Pothole claims its first victim.

Luposlipaphobia: The fear of being pursued by timber wolves around a kitchen table while wearing socks on a newly waxed floor.

"Now calm down there, ma'am. ... Your cat's gonna be fine
... just fine."

"Uh-oh."

People who don't know which end is up.

"Okay, before you go, let me read this one more time: 'Burn the houses, eliminate the townsfolk, destroy the crops, plunder their gold!' ... You knuckleheads think you can handle all that?"

Suddenly, his worst fears realized, the old fellow's tusks jammed.

At the Dog Comedy Film Festival

"Oh! Grog run into a ... a ... dang! Now which kind stick up and which kind hang down?"

The can of Mace lay where it had fallen from Bill's hand, and, for a moment, time froze, as each pondered the significance of this new development.

"No gophers, Stuart ... but there's an old garden rake of yours down here."

"For crying out loud, Norm. Look at you ... I hope I don't look half as goony when I run."

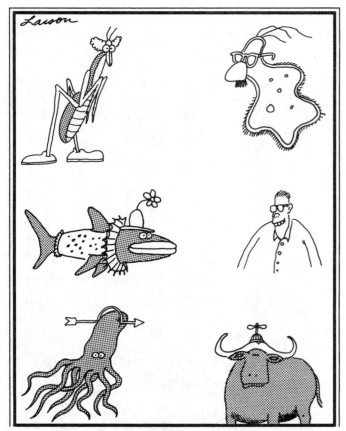

Clowns of the animal world

What dogs dream about

"You fool! 'Bring the honey,' I said. ... This isn't the same thing!"

When imprinting studies go awry

The mysterious, innate intuition of some animals

"OK, Baxter, if that's your game, I'll just reach over and push a few of *your* buttons."

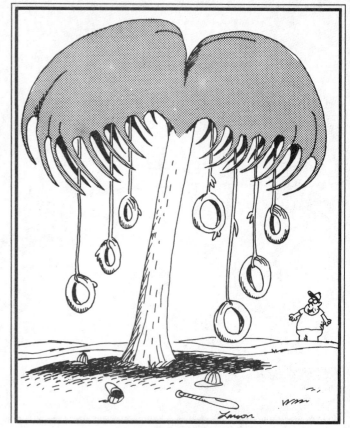

Her tentacles swaying seductively in the breeze, the Venus Kidtrap was again poised and ready.

"Sure, I'll draw, mister—but first you gotta say the magic word. ... Didn't your mother ever teach you the magic word?"

"Let's move it, folks ... Nothing to see here ... It's all over ... Move it along, folks ... Let's go, let's go ..."

"Play him, Sidney! Play him! ... Ooooooooweeeee! ... It's gonna be fresh burgers tonight!"

While the city slept, Dogzilla moved quietly from building to building.

Hannibal's first attempt

"Notice all the computations, theoretical scribblings, and lab equipment, Norm. ... Yes, curiosity killed these cats."

Seymour Frishberg: Accountant of the Wild Frontier

Confused by the loud drums, Roy is flushed into the net.

"No, Zak ... it Wilga's turn lick bowl."

"Oh c'mon now ... I know! Why don't you two go downstairs today and build a monster?"

At night, the forest custodians would arrive—sometimes stopping to laugh and gossip about the habits of certain daytime animals.

"Hey, Sid! Remember that time last summer we were all gathered around the kill like this, someone told a leopard joke, and you laughed so hard an antler came out of your nose?"

The first cruise arrow is tested.

"Dang! ... Sorry, buddy."

"Watch out for that tree, you idiot! ... And *now* you're on the wrong side of the road. Criminy! You're driving like you've been pithed or something."

Although an unexplained phenomenon, there is a place on the outskirts of Mayfield, Nebraska, where the sun does not shine.

"So what's this? I asked for a *hammer*! A hammer! *This* is a crescent wrench! … Well, maybe it's a hammer. … Damn these stone tools."

Natural selection at work

Creative dog writing

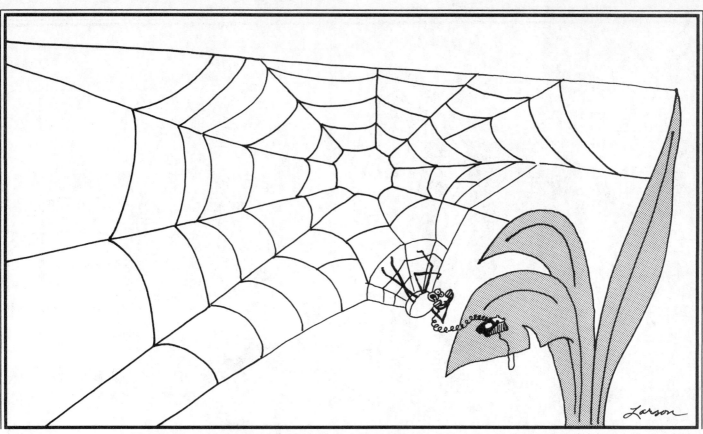

"Don't ask me how it happened, Stan ... just get your abdomen over here and get me unstuck!"

Jungle apparel

"Hey! Look at Red Bear! ... Waiiiiiiit ... THAT not real!"

Forest violence

Testing whether laughter IS the best medicine

Through patience and training, Professor Carmichael believed he was one of the few scientists who could freely visit the Wakendas.

Another sighting of the Loch Ness dog

"Hey! I'm coming, I'm coming—just cross your legs and wait!"

"Whoa, back off, Bobby Joe. That's just your reflection."

"Oh, no, he's quite harmless. ... Just don't show any fear. ... Squids can sense fear."

"Dennis, do you mind if Mrs. Carlisle comes in and sees your rhino tube-farm?"

Lost in the suburbs, Tonga and Zootho wander for days—plagued by dogs, kids, and protective mothers.

"Oo! ... Here he comes to feed on the milk of the living."

"Wait just a gol dang minute here! He's been dealin' from the bottom of the deck, Jake! My pappy always said, 'Never trust a grizzly.'"

"Well, I laid four Wednesday, three yesterday, and two more today ... of course, George keeps saying we shouldn't count them until they hatch."

"Sidney! I made a mistake! ... Deposit the $50 *check* into savings, and put the $500 in *cash* into checking!"

"Yes, yes, already, Warren! ... There IS film in the camera!"

The perils of improper circling

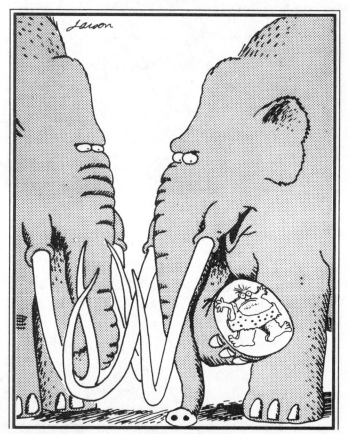

"Well, what the? ... I THOUGHT I smelled something."

"Well, this shouldn't last too long."

How birds see the world

"The boss wants his money, see? Or next time it
won't be just your living room we rearrange."

"Reuben! The Johnsons are here! You come up this instant ... or I'll get the hose!"

"Well, that cat's doing it again. Keeping that poor thing alive just to play with it awhile."

After reaching the far side, Tonga cut the bridge— sending the outraged suburbanites into the river below. Their idol was now his ... as well as its curse.

"Now this next slide, gentlemen, demonstrates the awesome power of our twenty megaton. ... For crying out loud! Not again!"

"Details are still sketchy, but we think the name of the bird sucked into the jet's engines was Harold Meeker."

And then Jake saw something that grabbed his attention.

"And *now* here comes Zubulu. If this isn't weird—middle of the night, and for some reason we're all restless."

"I've heard all kinds of sounds from these things, but 'yabba dabba doo' was a new one to me."

"Oh, this should be interesting. ... Looks as if your father has forgotten about the front window again."

"Varmints! ... You're all just a bunch of cheatin' varmints!"

"Is it still there?"

"Bob! Wake up! Bob! A ship! I think I see a ship! ... Where are your glasses?"

"I hate this place."

"Aw, c'mon, you guys—the cat's away and everyone's so dead serious."

"Trapped like rodentia!"

"No lions anywhere? ... Let me have the chair."

"Relax, Worthington. ... As the warm, moist air from the jungle enters the cave, the cool, denser air inside forces it to rise—resulting in turbulence that sounds not unlike heavy breathing."

"Doreen! There's a spider on you! One of those big, hairy, brown ones with the long legs that can move like the wind itself!"

"Hey, look. No. 1, we're closed, No. 2, I only work here, and No. 3, we don't like your kind in here anyway."

"Well, shoot. I just can't figure it out. I'm movin' over 500 doughnuts a day, but I'm still just barely squeakin' by."

"We'll ask you one more time, stranger—if you're *really* a cowboy from the Rio Grande, then why ain't your legs bowed or your cheeks tan?"

"Yes! That's right! The answer *is* 'Wisconsin!' Another 50 points for God, and ... uh-oh, looks like Norman, our current champion, hasn't even scored yet."

Testing whether or not animals "kiss"

"Listen. You want to be extinct? You want them to shoot and trap us into oblivion? ... *We're* supposed to be the animals, so let's get back out there and *act* like it!"

"No way. I'll put *my* magazine down when you put yours down."

"Mrs. Harriet Schwartz? This is Zathu Nananga of the Masai. ... Are you missing a little boy?"

Stimulus-response behavior in dogs

The third most common cause of forest fires

"Mr. Bailey? There's a gentleman here who claims an ancestor of yours once defiled his crypt, and now you're the last remaining Bailey and ... oh, something about a curse. Should I send him in?"

"Are you serious? Look at our arms! If anything, I'm *twice* as tan as you are."

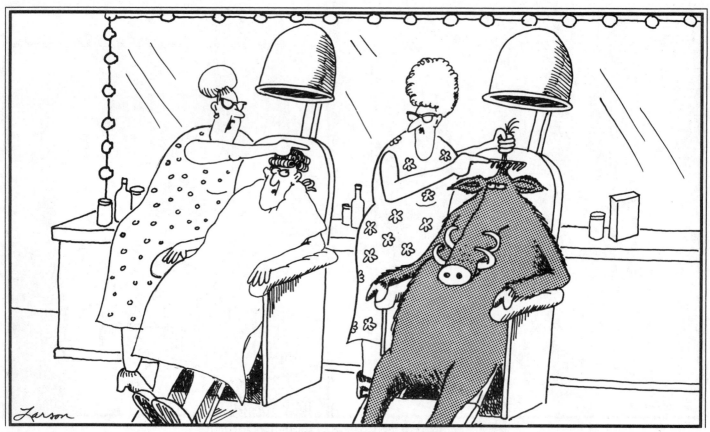

"Betty, you fool! Don't tease that thing!"

"My word! ... That one came just too close for comfort, if you ask me."

Between classes at the College of Laboratory Assistants

"Matthews ... we're getting another one of those strange
'aw blah es span yol' sounds."

"Dibs."

"Hors d'oeuvre?"

"OK, he's asleep. Pull the wagon, Buck, and I'll start
barkin' my head off ... God, I love this."

Stupid birds

Eventually, the chickens were able to drive a wedge
between Farmer Bob and Lulu.

"OK, one more time and it's off to bed for the both of
you. ... 'Hey, Bob. Think there are any bears in this old
cave?' ... 'I dunno, Jim. Let's take a look.'"

The Arnolds feign death until the Wagners, sensing the
sudden awkwardness, are compelled to leave.

"Eddie! I've told you a hundred times never to run with that through the house!"

"Quit complaining and eat it! ... Number one, chicken soup is good for the flu—and number two, it's nobody we know."